WILLIAMSBURG

TODAY & YESTERDAY

BY GRACE NORTON ROSÉ

WITH DRAWINGS BY JACK MANLEY ROSÉ

NEW YORK · G. P. PUTNAM'S SONS · MCMXXXX

Typography by Robert Josephy

To the illustrious men and women of yesterday who created Williamsburg in all its beauty and to those of today who made its restoration possible we dedicate this book.

ACKNOWLEDGMENTS: *To all of those who have aided us in the compilation of this book the author and the illustrator gratefully acknowledge their appreciation. To those who have written of Williamsburg as it was in the past and as it is today—particularly, the Reverend Hugh Jones, Lyon Gardiner Tyler, Lyman P. Powell, James Luther Kibler, Elsie Lathrop, Rutherfoord Goodwin, Dr. Hunter D. Farish, William Oliver Stevens, Arthur Shurcliff, and Dr. Earl G. Swem—thanks are due. We are especially grateful to the staffs of Williamsburg Restoration, Inc. and Colonial Williamsburg, Inc. for technical aid and for permission to reproduce a print of the Bodleian Plate; the College of William and Mary; the Bruton Parish Church; to Mr. and Mrs. Upton Beall Thomas, Jr. for their steadfast encouragement and undaunted assistance; and to Mr. William Graves Perry for his review of the illustrations and his helpful suggestions concerning them.*

CONTENTS

WILLIAMSBURG

TODAY & YESTERDAY

A BRIEF HISTORICAL SURVEY

WHEN IN 1699 the Royal Governor, Colonel Francis Nicholson, visualized and laid out the new capital of the Virginia Colony on that high ground between the rivers York and James known as the Middle Plantation, he was creating a little city that almost 230 years later was to have a new birth in nearly the same image.

The "noble great street six poles wide" which was named in honor of the Duke of Gloucester is now again the beautiful highway he intended it to be, and the others, including the two bearing his own name, once more take on the aspect of his vision.

Jamestown had more than once been wiped out. Pestilence, Indian massacre, and Bacon's Rebellion had taken heavy toll. Moreover, as it seemed unhealthily low-lying and malarial, the new site was chosen. Government and settlers moved eastward on the Peninsula to where the College of William and Mary had already been established by charter in 1693 through the efforts of the Reverend Dr. James Blair.

Behind a long palisade extending from creek to creek as a protection against Indian attacks the Governor proceeded to construct a more beautiful and better-

13

planned little city than many engineers and architects can erect today with all the elaborate means at their disposal.

With the lovely Christopher Wren-designed building of the College at one end of the fine street and the Capitol at the other less than a mile away, a splendid and hopeful start was made; and the years following saw that hope confirmed.

Up to the time of the Revolutionary War, Williamsburg continued to grow and grow charmingly. It became in a very few years a hospitable and lively town of red-brick and clapboarded homes, good taverns, and fine public buildings built in the dignified Colonial manner. The grand Palace for the Royal Governors, thought by some to reflect the influence of the Low Countries, was the crowning feature of the town's architectural loveliness.

The Ultramontane Expedition of the Knights of the Golden Horseshoe had its inception in Williamsburg under Governor Spotswood. The French and Indian Wars saw General Braddock and young Colonel George Washington in the King's uniform coming to and going from conferences in the Palace.

A long succession of Royal Governors, many of them beloved as well as respected, brought glamour and courtly gayety to the little capital. Guns sounded, illuminations blazed, and fireworks curved over the cupolas of the Palace and government buildings on the King's birthnights and on other celebrations. "The Gentm and Ladies here are perfectly well bred,—not an ill Dancer in my Govmt," wrote Governor Gooch to his brother concerning the elite of his colony. In the Court Church, known as the Bruton Parish Church, on the corner of Duke of Gloucester Street and the Palace Green, the Governors sat in state, and two were laid to their eternal rest under the stone flags of the aisles. Many of the traveled celebrities of the day in the New World came at some time to Williamsburg and wrote enthusiastically of the pomp and ceremony of the days while the Assembly was in session.

The faculty of the College was made up of the best minds available. George Wythe taught law to many a youngster destined to be among the leading statesmen of the new democracy. But the attempt at Indian education hardly justified itself; and soon this second oldest institution for higher education in America, became the training ground primarily for the masculine youth and quality of the Southern Colonies.

Theaters and horse racing flourished; and fairs, routs, and balls were held in connection with the meetings of the Assembly in the Capitol. There was much hard drinking, hard riding, dancing, and fine dressing indulged in by the blades and ladies of the day. Sedan chairs, coaches, and chaises swung along the "noble great street"; and fair ladies, in from the great houses on the James and York Rivers, glided across the brick sidewalks and folded their hoops through lovely Georgian doorways.

There were small manufactories; and many an artisan and professional man carried on his endeavors in a small building on his own house grounds; while Colonial businessmen gathered at the Exchange behind the turreted Capitol to carry on their financial transactions. Indians, black slaves, bound men and girls, redemptioners working out their passage money, soldiers of the King, trappers and frontiersmen, Virginia's own militia, tradespeople, tavern keepers, artisans, and craftsmen mingled on friendly if not quite equal terms with the statesmen, lawmakers, and wealthy planters of the outlying great places.

What is now a quiet, restful town, save for the influx of eager tourists who seem to bother it not at all, was before the Revolution and during it, surging with life and activity. Even after the capital had been moved to Richmond, Duke of Gloucester Street had incident and color. The Palace was a hospital for the wounded Americans; and French officers were quartered in the President's House of the College. But disastrous fires came rapidly, destroying forever valuable papers, rare furnishings, works of art, and buildings.

But what survived had the time-mellowed aura of the picturesque and the history-steeped past about it. The quiescence of the little town during the years after the Revolution enabled it to retain many of its original characteristics through the Civil War and the whole Victorian Era; and it survived into the twentieth century battered but still lovely.

However, the Reconstruction during which the South suffered so sorely brought excessive shabbiness and grievous dissolution. Also, the World War wrought a temporary change with activity centering about near-by munitions works. The curse of galvanized iron edifices and down-at-heel gas stations blossomed along Duke of Gloucester Street, as it was the direct route through to Norfolk.

One might quote from that quaint and lovely book entitled *A True Report Concerning Williamsburg in Virginia* by Rutherfoord Goodwin:

Some thirty Buildings of varying Nature and Design, ranging from a National Bank to a Pig Sty, had crowded together upon the Market Square to obscure the Powder Magazine and the Prison which had once commanded the southern Half of that ancient Common. Two School Houses, one a monstrous Structure, stood at the Head of the Palace Green, while a Dwelling of the Victorian Era closed what had been a Vista at its Foot. Two modern brick Stores occupied the Site of the Raleigh Tavern. The great Building of the College stood (after three Fires and as many Alterations) supported chiefly by Necessity and its own good Balance . . .

The Williamsburg of yesterday, a crumbling, war-scarred little city settling slowly through the generations into ruin or worse, holding a precious heritage of vast historical import, might today be living only with its memories, its traditions, its pride flickering ever and ever more faintly, as death, dissolution, and cheaper standards took their toll, but for the vision of one man, Doctor W. A. R. Goodwin, and the unstinted generosity of another, Mr. John D. Rockefeller, Jr.

The Frenchman's Map so-called, in the College Library, paced off and drawn by an unknown French officer of Rochambeau's engineers probably to while away the time, gave great impetus to Dr. Goodwin's vision. It checked street for street and building site for building site amazingly when the first exciting survey was made. Two students of William and Mary College under the architect William Graves Perry, working through the nights in the streets of Williamsburg, established locations and proved the accuracy of this map.

At that time the work of Restoration was hardly under way, but Dr. Goodwin was dreaming of a restored Colonial Capital and Mr. Rockefeller had come forward to make this dream possible. But neither students nor architect knew at that time the reason for the survey. In 1927 Mr. Rockefeller pledged his support, and the gradual acquiring of property began. Roughly 90 per cent of the original sites in the Colonial area have been taken over to date.

Great praise is due to the architects and the corps of earnest workers in all the activities of the Restoration and to all the delvers into Williamsburg's historic past. These fine men and devoted women have striven to make the vision and dream come to life, working with zeal and far-sightedness truly to re-create, to restore, and to cherish.

The Williamsburg of today, restored to the thrilling grandeur of its most vital and glamorous period, with few of the disadvantages and limitations of that era evident, is a place of peaceful serenity and of visual delight. Conjured from other times, manners, and customs, it is a rare town shedding the mellow contentment of a place well lived in, and well loved.

"That the Future May Learn from the Past" is the modern objective of this almost miraculous restoration of Colonial Williamsburg to its gracious eighteenth-century setting for the stirring events of history that took place upon these very streets.

WHEN THE CAPITAL was moved from Jamestown to Williamsburg in 1699, the General Assembly passed an act providing for the erection of a State House to be called the Capitol. On this "more salubrious site" 475 square feet were marked off for the Capitol, at the east end of Duke of Gloucester Street, commanding the town and opposite the handsome Wren-designed building of the College of William and Mary almost a mile down the fine road, which was "six poles wide." The General Assembly for the Colony used the College Building for its sessions until the "Government House" was ready for occupancy in 1705. Some years later the Reverend Hugh Jones, Chaplain to the Honorable Assembly, and a teacher of Mathematics in the College, wrote of it as the "best and most commodious Pile of its Kind" that he had ever seen or heard of.

Today it stands re-created as it was before the fire of 1747 destroyed it. However, the period selected by the Restoration planners for the city as a whole is roughly 1750; and by that time actually another less imposing edifice had replaced it, a pseudo-classic affair probably deserving the criticism Thomas Jefferson gave it in 1790. The decision to restore the original Capitol was undoubtedly a wise one. But the later building was really the one that witnessed the exciting happenings preceding the Revolution.

The General Assembly of Virginia met in the new building until the Capital was moved to Richmond in 1779. In later years the second building burned; and the site eventually became the property of the Association for the Preservation of Virginia Antiquities. The Association in turn presented it to Colonial Williamsburg Inc. for reconstruction. The fact that the crown glass of the windows and the large squarish floor tile of the reconstructed building came from the self-same factory and quarry in England which furnished these materials for the original structure more than 200 years ago gives a sense of historical continuity. Patrick Henry's portrait now hangs in the restored building whose original walls once echoed to his stirring peroration: "If this be Treason—make the most of it!" But perhaps the most interesting object is the original Speaker's chair from which the presiding officer rose to set at ease the stammering and blushing George Washington with these suave words, "Sit down, Mr. Washington—your modesty is equal to your valour; and that surpasses the power of any language I possess."

JACK MANLEY ROSE

THE CAPITOL

With the British Great Union streaming from its white cupola, this important building is almost immediately in evidence upon entering Williamsburg.

CLOSING THE VISTA at the end of the long Palace Green leading north from Duke of Gloucester Street, appears the Royal Governor's residence. It stands there unbelievably and absolutely satisfying, the culminating architectural design of Williamsburg. On Governor Nott's petition to house the Royal Governors of Virginia, this edifice was ordered built in 1705; and £3,000 were appropriated. So costly did it prove that it was called the Palace by the townspeople before it was finally completed some years later. However, repairs were made from time to time—paid for, it is said, by a two-shilling revenue tax collected on each hogshead of tobacco.

The Reverend Hugh Jones, professor of Mathematics at the College of William and Mary about 1722, wrote to London in this wise:

Upon Birth-Nights, and at Balls and Assemblies, I have seen as fine an Appearance, as good Diversion, and as splendid Entertainments . . . as I have seen anywhere else . . . and . . . stands of the best arms, nicely posited by the ingenious contrivance of the most accomplished Col. Spotswood.

Hereafter, during the "Publick Times" in the spring and fall, when the Assembly met, Williamsburg presented its gayest scene. The planters from the large river places opened their town houses for the social season. During these seasons of balls, dancing assemblies, dinners, the theater, and the races young George Washington often came to town and dined at the Palace.

A succession of Royal Governors, for the most part well-liked and kindly disposed toward the people of the little capital, took up their residence here until the troublous times at the outbreak of the Revolution forced Governor Dunmore to leave.

During and after the Yorktown Campaign the Palace served as a hospital for the wounded. The once-forgotten graves in the Palace Garden hold 156 Revolutionary soldiers. Governor Patrick Henry took up his abode here in 1776, but we have no very revealing records of his stay. Governor Thomas Jefferson also occupied it and jotted down notes of the floor plan of the Palace during his occupancy, a natural proceeding for a man with his interest in architecture. It burned in 1781 while still a hospital; and only the foundations and the flanking Office and Guard House remained until 1863, when these were pulled down by Union soldiers and the brick used in chimneys for officers' huts.

THE GOVERNOR'S PALACE

One slips back two centuries when glimpsing the gemlike Palace at the far end of the Palace Green, now appearing as it did when completed in 1749.

THE FLANKING BUILDINGS of the Palace proper — the Guard House and the Office—were undoubtedly very important in the Colonial scheme of things; but the Kitchen of the Palace played an equally significant part, although perhaps on a lower scale. Mighty trenchermen lived in the days of the Royal Governors. In England and also in America even a small dinner required considerable preparation. Great tureens of soup, a joint or a saddle of mutton at one end of the table and an eloquently poised and decorated fish at the other, a pair of capons and various small birds, with ices or a three-storied shape, or trifle, and sundry and suitable wines and condiments were taken for granted even at a modest dinner. All these were served from a kitchen across a courtyard, a feat which called for many house servants and kitchen helpers and a major domo with a head for detail and the precision of a drill sergeant. The procession of flunkies bearing great covered chafing dishes must have made the kitchen and the courtyard a beehive.

The careful inventories of the privately owned plate and dinner services of Governors Fauquier, Botetourt, and Dunmore give one an excellent idea of the lavish scale of these entertainments, which must have been a definite strain on the private purses of these gentlemen. On an official occasion, Governor Alexander Spotswood entertained 200 guests at supper and Governor Botetourt in 1769 wrote casually to London: ". . . 52 dined with me yesterday, and I expect at least that number to-day."

The addition, presumably in Governor Dinwiddie's time, of the Ball Room Wing and the lovely Chinese-influenced Supper Room, probably simplified the serving of meals and refreshments on such a gargantuan scale. Little seems to be handed down about the Governors' ladies and their Palace-keeping abilities. In fact one gets the impression from their letters that the Governors themselves did the ordering for the household.

It was from the inventories, the records and such archaeological remains as were recovered that the Palace was decorated and refurnished. The Restoration does not consider it quite complete. Indeed, as time goes on, old documents may shed light upon some controversy and a questioned piece be replaced with one whose relation to the Palace in Colonial times can go unchallenged. How very satisfactory it would be if it were possible to locate just the right sugar dish or the round mahogany table with leaves for the cook's room, according to Governor Botetourt's careful inventory, which is still preserved.

THE GOVERNOR'S PALACE: WEST YARD

This intimate vista recalls the time when a beloved Royal Governor tactfully hid political differences beneath a "Display of Social Serenity."

FLANKING THE PALACE on the east side and balancing the Guard House on the other is the building known as the Governor's Office. After the Palace burned in 1781, both the office and the Guard House were used as private dwellings and were pulled down during the occupation of Williamsburg by Union troops.

The Palace boasted a well to the east and one to the west. Great fireplaces heated the rooms, and somewhere in the East Yard or in the West Yard huge stacks of firewood must have been stored against the damp and chilly winter months. The generous chimneys of the Tidewater Country are especially noticeable here over the steep roof lines. Soaring above them, the white cupola dominates the stately tree tops.

Even before the capital was moved from Jamestown to Williamsburg, each Royal Governor bore with him when he came from England, instructions to build a Governor's House. It was not until Governor Nott's brief and crowded administration, however, that the work got under way. After Nott's death the building operations were supervised by President Edmund Jennings.

In all for seventy-six years the social and political life of the Colony bowed in and out of the Palace portals. Over muddy country roads, through sandy stretches, in coaches, many of them imported from Europe, and on fine American-bred horses, came the landed gentry from the countryside to pay their respects to Their Majesties' representatives during the Court Sessions and on gala occasions.

The actual foundations of both of the main building and "Numerous dependencies" were discovered when the Palace site was excavated many years later by the Restoration. The Bodleian Print furnished a glimpse of the front elevation of the building. Also Thomas Jefferson's data, preserved by the Massachusetts Historical Society, and the Frenchman's Map, owned by the College of William and Mary, shed much light on the appearance of the main buildings. So it was that when the Restoration work was really begun much documentary evidence was in the hands of the Research Department. Where real evidence was not available, Colonial Virginian and English precedents were consulted.

In its day, the Palace doubtlessly served as an example and an inspiration to the builders of many of the great Virginia country houses of the first half of the eighteenth century.

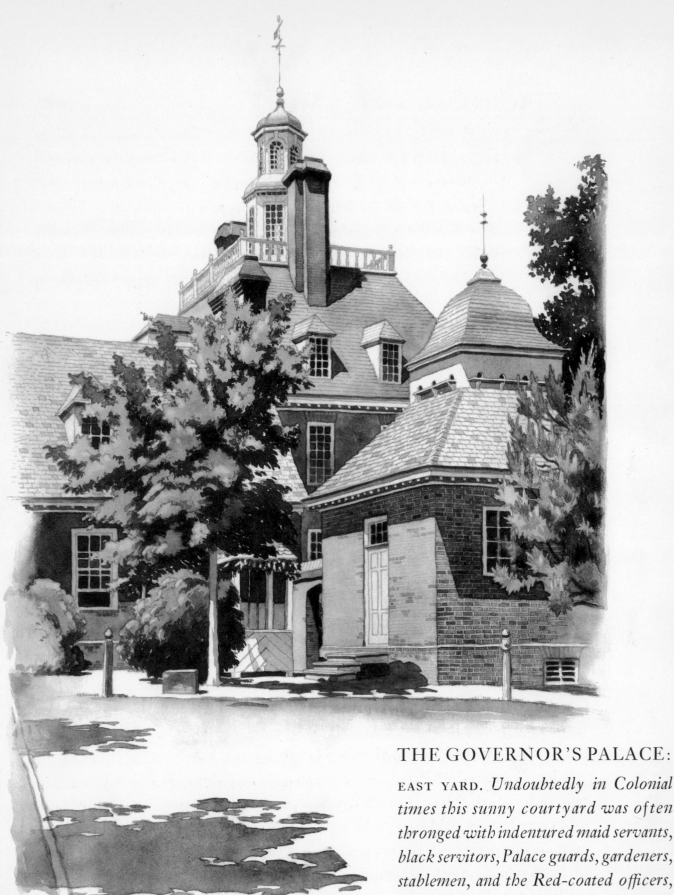

THE GOVERNOR'S PALACE:

EAST YARD. *Undoubtedly in Colonial times this sunny courtyard was often thronged with indentured maid servants, black servitors, Palace guards, gardeners, stablemen, and the Red-coated officers, who in Dunmore's regime were called "Montague's boiled crabs".*

SURROUNDING THE PALACE were 360 acres of approaches, gardens, and park. The design has been restored either according to the evidence of original documents or the information obtained from excavations on the site. The Bodleian Print and old maps indicated the general plan and the position of the walls. This enabled the excavators to lay bare the foundations, the steps, the transverse axis, the outbuildings, the separate levels, the vinery garden, and the terraces. The Canal and the Governor's Fish Pond were found to need little more restoration than the rebuilding of the dam at the lower end.

English designs of a slightly earlier period gave valuable guidance to the restorers, but for the actual plantings Colonial Virginian precedents were followed whenever possible. So effectively has the work been done that a tract of land which ten years ago contained railroad tracks, a factory, and several school buildings is now one of the most elaborate and beautiful gardens in America.

This is an ideal spot for anyone interested in painting, sketching, reading, or just pure relaxation. Chuckling laughter from colored boys in Colonial dress clipping hedges or working overhead in the pleached alleys comes only faintly to the ears and seems to blend with the Southern charm of unaccustomed bird songs. Occasionally, shrill voices do break the solitude, as a small group of real tourists trail by, telling about other gardens they have seen or known; but the interruption cannot dispel more than momentarily the atmosphere of serenity which mantles the landscape.

The names of the principal features of the grounds themselves give some idea of the spaciousness of the whole: The Twelve Apostles, cedar trees trimmed like yews; the formal Ballroom Garden; the North Garden; the long Bowling Green with its raised terraces at either end; the Ice House and Mount; the Fruit Garden; the Revolutionary Soldiers' Graveyard; the West, or Kitchen, Yard; the Kitchen garden; and the Hanging Gardens.

The Palace is the last and most extensive of the Exhibition Places to see, and one is wise to give over a separate day to it and its gardens alone. No matter how often one returns to the scene he is ever and again newly impressed with the cunning and artistry of the landscaping.

The white cupola surmounting the Palace, the pale salmon-orange of the walls, and the blue-gray slate of the roofs contrast exquisitely with the green of the gardens, all combining into an unforgettable picture of serenity and elegance.

THE PALACE GARDENS

When the doors of the Chinese-influenced Supper Room are thrown open, you are invited to enjoy the Gardens spread out before you.

THE REVEREND JAMES BLAIR, who was appointed Commissary of the Bishop of London in Virginia in 1689, first started agitating for a Free School, or College, before the General Assembly at the Jamestown settlement. The Assembly accepted his propositions and sent him to England to raise the funds for a college and to secure its charter. Although he waited on Their Majesties William and Mary for two years before the Charter was granted, he was by no means idle. He managed to have a part of the income from certain estate funds left by the Honorable Robert Boyle "for pious and religious uses" assigned to the College of William and Mary for the education of Indian children.

The foundations of the Sir Christopher Wren Building were laid at the Middle Plantation in 1695, four years before the capital was moved from Jamestown to the newly laid-out town of Williamsburg. Hugh Jones, our frequently quoted annalist, wrote of it in 1724:

... "first modelled by Sir Christopher Wren, adapted to the Nature of the Country by the Gentlemen there; and since it was burnt down, it has been rebuilt, and nicely contrived, altered and adorned by the ingenious Direction of General Spotswood; and is not altogether unlike Chelsea Hospital."

To Governor Spotswood, whose rare, restrained taste and energetic interest in architecture is evident in the survivals of early Williamsburg, considerable credit should go for preserving the Wren tradition.

A long walk broken only by the battered and moss-stained marble statue of Lord Botetourt, Royal Governor of the Colony from 1768 to 1770 and patron of the College, leads to the simple, impressive entrance of this, the main building. The Chapel and the Great Hall form the side wings to the rear. Three visitations of fire, usually through carelessness, have wrecked this lovely building from time to time. It served as a hospital for French troops in 1781, and during the Civil War it was used as a barracks for Confederate soldiers and as a Confederate hospital. After the war it was finally rebuilt, in spite of the College's straitened circumstances. Recently it has been completely restored.

Constantly improving its faculty and its prestige, the College now has become progressive and also coeducational, thereby fulfilling the pious thought of its well-wisher Hugh Jones, who in his famous book declared it to be a great pity that the education of girls should be so neglected at Williamsburg and other towns in the New Colony.

THE CHRISTOPHER WREN BUILDING

OF THE COLLEGE OF WILLIAM AND MARY

It seems to be well established that Sir Christopher Wren drew in London the plans of this "beautiful and commodious building".

THE CHAPEL LIES in the southwest wing of the Christopher Wren Building and is now restored to its original condition in 1729-32. This Chapel, handsomely paneled and adorned with classic tablets to the famous men buried beneath its stone-flagged floor, is used for the weekly nondenominational services of the College. The arms of George I and II are displayed over the Gallery.

It was originally intended that the building should form two sides of a quadrangle, but this plan was never completed. The Chapel, to the southwest, and the Great Hall in the northwest wing, are connected by an arcade upon the walls of which are the marble tablets commemorating historical episodes in the history of the College and the outstanding alumni concerned with the history of the country in the Revolutionary days. George Washington received his first public office as surveyor from the College and later became Chancellor of the institution.

The Great Room, paneled in native pine and balancing the Chapel, is similar in design and identical in size. It was used for meetings of the General Assembly while the new Capitol at the opposite end of Duke of Gloucester Street was in process of construction.

Buried beneath the flagging of the Chapel are Sir John Randolph and his sons, John, the Tory, and Peyton, the Patriot; Bishop James Madison; Chancellor Robert Nelson; and Lord Botetourt.

The College was the first in America to receive a charter from the Crown, dated 1693, under seal of the Privy Council. It was obliged by the terms of the charter to give two sets of Latin verses to the Governor every fifth day of November as quit rent for its land. The famous Ultramontane Expedition of the Knights of the Golden Horseshoe, led by Governor Spotswood to the Valley of the Shenandoah in 1716, was celebrated in classic lines composed by the Reverend Arthur Blackamore, Professor of the Grammar, or Classical School, on the following rent day. It was also the first and only American college to receive its coat of arms from the College of Heralds in London. This coat of arms was granted in 1694 and used for many years until the seal was lost or destroyed and another one designed locally was substituted. Recently the design for the original seal was discovered in the College of Heralds in London by Dr. J. A. C. Chandler, President of the College from 1919 to 1934. A replica of the first seal is now in the vaults of the College Library.

JACK MANLEY ROSÉ

INTERIOR OF THE CHAPEL

THE CHRISTOPHER WREN BUILDING

Aided by a copperplate engraving discovered in the Bodleian Library, the Restoration was able to reconstruct more exactly the wings of the Christopher Wren Building.

THE CURTSEYING of the girls and the doffing of round Freshman caps by the boys before the statue of Norborne Berkeley, Baron de Botetourt, goes on each fall until the winning of the big football game of the season or the arrival of Christmas vacation suspends all Freshman rules.

These honors do not seem excessive when we see the inscriptions which the General Assembly of Virginia ordered engraved on the pedestal of the statue. One reads:

> *Let wisdom and justice preside in any country*
> *The people will rejoice and must be happy.*

The other proclaims:

> *America, behold your friend,*
> *Who, leaving his native country,*
> *Declined those additional honors which*
> *Were there in store for him that*
> *He might heal your wounds and restore*
> *Tranquillity and happiness to this*
> *Extensive continent   With what zeal*
> *And anxiety he pursued these glorious*
> *Objects,   Virginia thus bears her*
> *Grateful testimony.*

The statue was originally set up in the piazza of the Capitol. The very flagstone upon which it stood has been located by the Restoration, and a railed-off space is hopefully reserved to receive it once again, although it may be a rather difficult and delicate matter for the Restoration to persuade the College authorities to part with it now.

Although it was treasured by the House of Burgesses, hoodlums, probably urged on by patriotic intent, knocked it from its pedestal during the later years of the Revolution; and it lay broken and battered until the College bought it for a small sum. It now stands moss-streaked and mellow against the satisfying background of the Wren entrance.

This amiable piece of English sculpture by Richard Hayward was intended to commemorate "those many public and social virtues of the Governor which so eminently adorned his illustrious character." He was buried in the Chapel of the College, where his remains still rest.

LORD BOTETOURT

*To this Royal Governor and Patron the
Freshmen of the College of William and
Mary pay their respects as they pass.*

FOR MANY YEARS this structure contained the first permanent school in America for teaching Indian children. Now it houses the Faculty Club and has accommodations for occasional distinguished visitors. It is one of the three original buildings on the Campus of the College of William and Mary, and corresponds in general design to the President's House facing it. Although it is nine years older, it was also probably built by Henry Cary. Established and supported by charity funds devised by the Honorable Robert Boyle, the English scientist, and invested in the Brafferton Estate, the building continued as an Indian School until the Revolution.

Hugh Jones had to say of it and of Indian Education in general in his *Present State of Virginia* published in London in 1724:

The Indians who are upon Mr. Boyle's Foundation have now a handsom Apartment for themselves and their Master, built near the College . . .

The young Indians, procured from the tributary or foreign Nations with much Difficulty, were formerly boarded and lodged in the Town; where abundance of them used to die, either thro' Sickness, change of Provision, and way of Life, or as some will have it, often for want of proper Necessaries and due Care taken with them. Those of them that have escaped well, and have been taught to read and write, have for the most Part returned to their Home, some with and some without Baptism, where they follow their own savage Custom and heathenish Rites. . . .

But 'tis great Pity that more Care is not taken about them, after they are dismissed from School.

Governor Alexander Spotswood's own Indian School at Christanna near the Meherrin River was discontinued and its Master, the Reverend Charles Griffin, became Master of the Brafferton School.

While sojourning in the Brafferton, Spotswood himself made his will there, leaving all his books and mathematical instruments to the College. This was a magnanimous act, since President James Blair was almost constantly laboring to have him relieved of his post as Governor.

At one time during the Civil War the Federal officer commanding the forces occupying Williamsburg made the Brafferton his headquarters. After the war it was left forlorn and empty, its echoes roused only by the pathetic peals evoked from the Wren tower by the "old Bell-Ringer," President Ewell, who kept the charter of the College for posterity until aid was forthcoming.

34

JACK MANLEY ROSE

THE BRAFFERTON

THE COLLEGE OF WILLIAM AND MARY

Young Indian braves, persuaded to attend the College that they might become missionaries to their own people, were housed here with their Master.

HENRY CARY, famous builder of Williamsburg edifices in the eighteenth century, built this severe and somewhat stately house in 1732. Today it is lovelier than it ever has been, with its irregular but formal little front garden facing the Richmond Road and its simple south façade caressed by flickering shadows from the fine old trees of the Campus.

It is slightly larger than the Brafferton, facing it on the opposite side of the path leading to the Christopher Wren Building. In 1931 the Restoration swept away a large front porch and other excrescences and restored it to its original design.

We learn something of the economics of Colonial education from this statement written by Hugh Jones in 1724: "The Salary of the President Mr. James Blair has lately been ordered reduced from £150 to £100 1. per ann." The President also was provided with a garden "suitable to his position."

In 1734 the Legislature gave the College for the remainder of the term of twenty-one years the whole of the duty of one penny per gallon on liquors, provided that some part thereof should be spent on books. A book with the printed label *The Gift of the General Assembly of Virginia in the Year 1734* has been preserved.

In 1754 board at the College was £13 per session. Fifteen of the seventy-five resident lads were on scholarships. Eight of the wealthiest students had Negro boys to wait on them. Eight of the remainder were Indians.

However "suitably" the Presidents were housed, some complaint was made of the professors' methods of living. At one time two Reverend Doctors who were married kept, "contrary to all rules of seats of learning, their wives, children and servants in college which occasioned much confusion and disturbance."

The Reverend James Blair, the first President, obtained £300 in London to erect the building from pirates whose seized property was returned to them on condition they make this donation. It has served at least eighteen Presidents of the College of William and Mary.

In June and July 1781, in the days preceding the Battle of Green Springs, it became the headquarters of Lord Cornwallis. After the Yorktown Campaign it was accidentally burned while occupied by members of Rochambeau's Medical Staff. It has the distinction of having been repaired and refurnished with money from the General Fund of the French Army.

THE PRESIDENT'S HOUSE

This house has shared practically every vicissitude of fortune that has come to the College: from the Revolution through the hard Civil War era to the present period of progress and advancement.

THERE WAS already a brick church belonging to the Bruton Parish located on land donated by Colonel John Page, when the New Capital, Williamsburg, was laid out at Middle Plantation in 1699. But by 1706 the cost of repairs to this church, built probably in the Gothic style, had become so great that the vestry ordered that a new one be built. Governor Alexander Spotswood came to the rescue with plans and additional financing so that by 1715 this Court Church of Colonial Virginia was practically completed. But, as it has remained in use all these years, various additions have been made from time to time.

The Colonial aspect of the interior of the Church was destroyed in 1840 by an entire rearrangement of the floor plan. The Reverend W. A. R. Goodwin and the architect, Mr. J. Stewart Barney, partially reconditioned it in 1905-07. The restoration was completed recently with the aid of Colonial Williamsburg Inc., Williamsburg Restoration, Inc., and certain funds collected by Dr. Goodwin from friends of the Parish.

Within the yard and within the Church are many interesting stone tablets and slabs, a number dating from the seventeenth century. Two Governors, an acting Governor, Councillors, Attorney Generals, Judges, Doctors, and many unknown Confederate soldiers are buried there.

One of the oldest mural tablets in America, a rubbing of which is shown, is to Daniel Parke, one-time Secretary of the Colony of Virginia and one of his Majesty's Councillors, who "dyed ye 6th of March Anno 1679." Many graves of early date bear no markers. It is said that at one time the Sexton received ten pounds of tobacco for each grave dug.

Stirring conversations have taken place in the old Church vestibule, along with gay chatter, neighborly solicitude, and whispered gossip. Not the least exciting times have been these later days of the Restoration. It is said that often in this vestibule Dr. Goodwin became so enthusiastic and interested in persuading certain parishioners to sell to the Restoration that one of the choir members would have to come to tell him that the congregation was assembled and waiting.

It must have been of the utmost satisfaction to this man to see his dream of Old Williamsburg Restored come so amazingly true. It was his devotion to this vision that persuaded Mr. Rockefeller to give of his vast wealth to this marvelous undertaking.

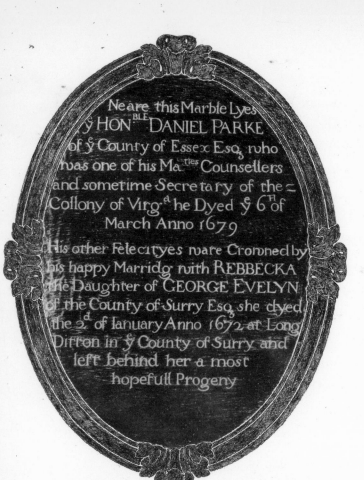

Neare this Marble Lyes
y HON^{BLE} DANIEL PARKE
of y County of Essex Esq who
was one of his Maties Counsellers
and sometime Secretary of the
Collony of Virg^d he Dyed y 6th of
March Anno 1679

His other Felecityes ware Crowned by
his happy Marridg with REBBECKA
the Daughter of GEORGE EVELYN
of the County of Surry Esq she dyed
the 2^d of January Anno 1672 at Long
Ditton in y County of Surry and
left behind her a most
hopefull Progeny

BRUTON PARISH CHURCH

*Governor Alexander Spotswood, Royal
Governor of Virginia, furnished the
plans for this church. It was completed
in 1715, and its exterior is largely original.*

JACK MANLEY ROSÉ

GEORGE WASHINGTON worshipped in this Church when he was in Williamsburg. His name appears eleven times on the Parish register of baptisms. The Interior is now lovely with its pale oyster-colored walls and woodwork, its clear glass windows, and the gray-green flags of its stone floor. No longer does the velvet canopy hang over the Governor's pew; only a stately chair is there now. And the pulpit, rising over the congregation, and looking down upon the box pews, is immeasurably more impressive with its dark rich woodwork gleaming against the pale walls. The canopy, or sounding board, over the pulpit, is of dark wood also, as are the chancel rail and the coping of the pews. Candle stands of graceful Colonial design adorn the pulpit, and tiny pricks of diffused starlight gleam through the ceiling.

The Church is always hospitable to the visitor on weekdays as well as on Sundays, and there is a sympathetic sexton on hand to act as guide. The ideal way to absorb the mellow atmosphere so rich in historic association is to attend the leisurely candlelight service.

Of the three ancient silver Communion Sets, the two sketched include the oldest one, from the Jamestown Church, and the one given in the time of King George III. A third was willed in 1773 to the College of William and Mary by Lady Gooch, the Colonial Governor's wife.

The interior of the tower holds much of the feeling of the ruined Jamestown Church. In it hangs the Liberty Bell of Virginia, given to the Parish by James Tarpley in 1761. The Baptismal Font, tradition says, was brought from the Church at Jamestown to the Bruton Church. It has been associated in local folk-tales with the baptism of Pocahontas, although without foundation in fact.

Both inside and outside, this building has the unmistakable stamp of authenticity about it. Sun-flecked brick sidewalks lead the eye naturally to low brick walls over which the shadows of the trees pour; and through the leaves appears the mellow church surrounded by the venerable tombs of those who helped to build it. Among them lies one tomb not yet so venerable, the tomb of one whose real monument is this dream city of Restored Williamsburg—the Rev. W. A. R. Goodwin. Even Mr. Rockefeller, whose vast generosity and far-sighted patriotism gave this dream substance and reality, could ask for no greater reward than that this monument, in which they both share, should be a source of joy, of beauty of living, and of historical import to the ages to come.

BRUTON PARISH
CHURCH, INTERIOR

This church was built as the Court Church of Colonial Virginia. In 1840 its interior was altered. Restoration was partially effected in 1906 and is now complete.

GOVERNOR BOTETOURT signed an act authorizing the erection of this building, centrally located on Duke of Gloucester Street, for the joint use of the City of Williamsburg and the County of James City. It replaced an earlier county courthouse deemed inadequate, the site of which, across the Market Square on Francis Street, is now occupied by a new group of buildings incorporating the original foundations and one chimney. This newest courthouse contains both the City court and the courts under the jurisdiction of the County.

The eighteenth-century building in the Wren tradition sketched here, was damaged by a fire confined mostly to the interior in 1911, and was not finally restored until 1932. The records were saved, and The Court House plan was preserved, but all the appurtenances of the Court were removed. The architects decided for the sake of authenticity to omit the columns that were intended in 1770 to support the center gable but which never reached their destination.

The Court House had been in continuous use up to the time of the Restoration and now serves as a museum for the Restoration's Archaeological Exhibit.

THE BODLEIAN PLATE

THE OLD COURT HOUSE

The Court House has been in use from 1770 to the time of the Restoration. It now houses the fascinating Archaeological Museum.

After the foundations of a Colonial house had been identified, measured, and excavated, every shovelful of earth was removed and sifted. Any interesting fragments of household utensils were plotted, cleaned, catalogued, and placed on exhibition. Examination of such a resultant mass of bits of ware, utensils, and even shoes gives one a fairly clear picture of the scale of living in Colonial America, which is thrilling to those to whom the reconstructing of this particular American scene is vivid and captivating.

This excavated material, most interesting to all students of Americana, bears close inspection. It contributed so largely to the genuineness of the research necessary to the rebuilding and furnishing of the Exhibition Buildings that anyone about to view them should see this collection.

THE DRAWING OF the original Raleigh Tavern in Benson J. Lossing's *Field Book of the Revolution* differs only slightly from the new building that the Restoration has erected upon the old foundations.

This most famous of Virginiaia taverns was closely tied up with the life of the capital in the days of the Virginia Colony's greatest glory, and so many important and historic episodes took place within its hospitable walls that it was rightly called the very "Cradle of Liberty."

It was built some time before 1742, but we do not know by whom. However, it was always fortunate in its hosts, who conducted it with every degree of comfort and elegance. Notable among them was Henry Wetherburn, whose "biggest bowl of arrack punch" was once bartered for two hundred acres of land.

The Apollo Room of the Tavern knew lively times both social and political. Here the men and women of the Colony met at balls and routs during the sessions of the General Assembly and Courts. It was here that young red-haired Thomas Jefferson danced with and lost his "lovely Belinda." Here too was held the first meeting of the Phi Beta Kappa Society, which was founded by students of the College of William and Mary on December 5, 1776.

When in May, 1769, Norbourne Berkeley, Baron de Botetourt, then Governor, was obliged to dissolve the Assembly, the Burgesses promptly repaired to "the Apollo"; and with Peyton Randolph acting as moderator adopted a nonimportation agreement. After Governor Dunmore had dissolved the House of Burgesses for showing sympathy over the closing of the port of Boston, "An association" was signed in the Raleigh by George Washington,

Peyton Randolph, Thomas Jefferson, Patrick Henry, and eighty-five others.

During the Revolution the Tavern served as a brilliant background for General Washington's birthday balls, dinners for departing Continental officers and visiting French ones, auctions of prize ships and confiscated loyalist property, routs, state functions, and even courts martial.

After the capital was transferred to Richmond in 1779, the Tavern still continued active until the close of the Revolution. Then the Tavern and the city alike settled into dignified inactivity broken only by the visit of the Marquis de Lafayette in 1824 and a brief building boom preceding the Civil War. The Tavern burned to the ground in 1859; and only the original stone base of the leaden bust of Sir Walter Raleigh over the door survives and is now a part of the Exhibition at the Old Court House.

THE RALEIGH TAVERN

This Tavern, dedicated to "Jollity—the offspring of wisdom and good living—" was the scene of many political meetings, informal and otherwise, preceding the Revolution.

THIS BUILDING was popularly known for many years as the Poor Debtor's Prison, but it was really the County Jail for all classes of prisoners. It still stands on property adjacent to the Market Square. At one time not very long ago it was overshadowed by a large brick addition which, together with the Baptist Church, a livery stable, and many indeterminate buildings of hasty construction, helped to obscure it and the little Public Magazine as well. The Magazine, however, is not one of the Restoration buildings; but is owned by the Association for the Preservation of Virginia Antiquities.

In the past it must have been close to the actual common life of the Colonial period. Markets were held on the Square, which it faces, at least bi-weekly during certain periods of the town's history, as well as two annual fairs, one, of course, during the time of the Assembly and Court Sittings, and the other at the discretion of the city authorities. These were "Publick Times," and they brought into Williamsburg the gentry and their retinues from the great places on the James and York Rivers and the surrounding country generally. Cock fighting, foot races, singing for a book of Ballads as a prize, or dancing for a pair of handsome shoes and stockings—the popular amusements on such occasions—presumably took place then.

Probably all was quiet at the Prison on April 20, 1775, and the prisoners deep in slumber, when at Dunmore's orders, men under Lieutenant Collins from His Majesty's armed schooner the *Magdalen* removed the fifteen half-barrels of powder from the Powder Magazine to the *Fowey*, man-of-war, and so set off the fuse that ignited the smoldering spirit of Virginia.

Now, in appearance the Prison is much like a small private house, quite in keeping with its neighbors of the Restoration, although it is privately owned. Shuttered and boarded up when last observed, it seemed less attractive than at the time when sketched. The low fence around it, the lamp post, and the simple door-yard planting give it a quaint look of withdrawal from the present and invest it with the authentic atmosphere of the eighteenth century. Its chimney is broad and comfortable, and the vines that drape it today add considerably to its picturesque quality.

The Daughters of the American Revolution now use this structure upon occasion. It retains much of the character of the private dwelling it once was before it became the county jail.

THE COLONIAL PRISON

Known variously as the Debtors' Prison, the County Jail, and the General Prison, it was used "on sufferance" by the City of Williamsburg for a time.

THIS WAS THE town house of Colonel Ludwell, who became the third husband of Governor Sir William Berkeley's widow, she who insisted upon always being called Lady Berkeley, even on her tombstone.

John Paradise, of London, married Lucy Ludwell, the Colonel's granddaughter. The Paradises entertained largely in London the literary Club of Dr. Samuel Johnson, Oliver Goldsmith, and Sir Joshua Reynolds. Even then Lucy Ludwell Paradise began to show evidences of eccentricity. After her husband's death she returned to her native town and took up her residence in this fine mansion, called by the Restoration a typical home of the gentry in eighteenth-century Williamsburg.

There is a story about a Lucy Paradise, though it is not known whether it was the same Lucy, which recounts that when meeting George Washington at an assembly for the first time she was so impressed she berated and belabored her husband because he was so small and ugly.

It was said that Lucy Paradise kept her coach indoors and that callers were invited to sit with her in it as it was rolled to and fro by colored servants. A Negro page with a bonnet on a cushion attended her when she went abroad on the streets of the little city in a towering coiffure. A pleasant little habit of pouring scalding water on gentlemen whom she didn't favor when they happened in for tea was attributed at first to her fashionable sojourn in England. But eventually it became clear that her mind was deranged and she was removed to the Hospital for the Insane.

At her death the litigation involving the estate brought her grandson Philip, the son of the Italian Count Barziza, of Venice, to Williamsburg. Here he spent the rest of his years in futile lawsuits, admiration of the ladies of the Colony, criticism of their dwellings, and in the begetting of ten children, the last of which was known as Decimus Ultimus Barziza.

This house at present is much as it was when the Restoration took it over. Today it houses an exhibition of American Folk Art presented by Mrs. John D. Rockefeller, Jr. Ships' figureheads and tin trays, hitching posts and looking-glass frames, weather vanes and velvet paintings, and silks and shell creations are here displayed. These varied articles give one an excellent idea of the handicrafts of the time and the ladylike pursuits of the fair sex during the era preceding and following the Revolution.

JACK MANLEY ROSE

THE LUDWELL-PARADISE HOUSE

After the Revolution an eccentric mistress of this house, Lady Paradise self-styled, made her home a social center of the time.

HERE AND THERE in the gardens surrounding the houses the indispensable mechanisms of the domestic economy—kitchens, smoke houses, well heads, wood sheds, milk houses, stables, etc. —are to be glimpsed through the enveloping shrubbery. Incredibly canny planting has draped native wistaria vines over white-painted well houses, massed great clumps of boxwood where its dark rich value is needed to set off the delicate spraying of mimosa or flowering dogwood. Espaliered fruit trees break the length of walls, and holly hedges in their thorny trigness confine the more exuberant growths. All of this has been arranged to perfection in the Ludwell-Paradise gardens.

Beyond the Kitchen sketched are the stables, now holding the four horses and the antique phaeton and post chaise owned by the Restoration. These are used daily, except in inclement weather, to carry the charming hostesses in their hoops and lace caps to their duties as cicerones in the buildings open to the public. The dark green post chaise with its delicate lining and silken panels, built in the Adam period of 1765-1780, and the blue phaeton, open and lighter of weight, were both originally owned by Colonial Virginians.

Many of the kitchens in restored Williamsburg are now being rented as living quarters, studios, offices, and guest houses. The income from these buildings, unless they are privately owned, goes back into upkeep and the fund for educational and historical purposes.

In the original city plan it was provided that each householder should own not less than a half-acre plot. These half-acre plots allowed ample space for flower gardens, box-lined walks, vegetable gardens, beds of herbs and simples, small fruits, and even a tiny orchard, all grouped about the white-washed out-buildings, of which the kitchen was usually the most important and the largest.

Also these ample spaces between the buildings served as effective fire breaks, which was an important consideration in Colonial Williamsburg, as there was no fire-fighting system according to modern standards. It is reassuring to know that now under the Restoration all these historic buildings are fireproofed and protected by a good fire company and an adequate water supply.

On some lots the office or workshop had the place of honor, but at the Ludwell-Paradise House, which was the town residence of gentlemen of leisure, undoubtedly the accent was upon the Coach House, the Pleasure Gardens, and the Kitchen.

50

THE LUDWELL-PARADISE KITCHEN

This building and the Stables at the end of the garden saw great activity in the eighteenth century.

MARKET SQUARE
TAVERN YARD

JACK MANLEY ROSÉ

STANDING NORTH of the Capitol, this old place is inspected with interest by the ever-increasing stream of sight-seers who take the footpath from the Capitol across the fields to the Gaol. Rising out of great clumps of dark, glistening boxwood, the gable end of the oldest part is dominated by the sturdy and enormous chimney. This, the most westerly section, was possibly built by the grandson of Richard Coke.

The extensive gardens were an early landmark and are so designated on the Court Records of York County just after the Revolution. They are now thoroughly rehabilitated and are a privilege to see at any season. The autumn crocuses, for instance, of a size quite bewildering to the Northern visitor, range from pale yellow to deep orange, and from a faint lavender to a rich purple. The vistas stretch out before one, green, inviting, and mossy, apparently of great age and certainly of great artistry. The rose garden is particularly noteworthy.

What has been produced in the little town by the blending of architecture and landscaping fills one constantly with amazement. But the full measure of accomplishment can only be appreciated by those who have watched the systematic working out of this very comprehensive scheme from the beginning.

This property was among the first to be partially renovated by the Restoration—in 1928—while Miss Lottie Garrett was still living.

Two generations of students of the College of William and Mary remember the pleasant Sunday teas that they enjoyed in this fine old house with Miss Lottie as their delightful hostess. She kept open house for the student body and long continued the fine old tradition of solidarity between the college and the town. It is to be hoped that the future generations of boys and girls of the College will again be welcomed to that house so replete in the past with the charm of graceful Southern hospitality.

The rare old landscape wall paper for years greatly interested experts in interior decorating because of its unfaded blue design. A desk, said to have belonged to Governor Yeardley or to his wife, Temperance Flowerdew, of the Jamestown Colony, has always been an object of intense speculation because the secret drawer or compartment it was reputed to have surely had has never been located.

At the east end of the house is a little classic office building, well-screened with rose vines, probably built by Dr. Robert Major Garrett.

THE COKE-GARRETT HOUSE

John Coke, a jeweler and maker of ladies' crystal bobs, earrings, and patch boxes, lived in this house after 1755.

ODAY THE PUBLIC GAOL is fresh and clean; the walls are hung with Hogarth engravings; and a plump and smiling Gaoler greets the visitor at the door. Indeed it is hard to imagine that this was the dreaded prison for the Colony and later the Commonwealth of Virginia for a period of seventy-five years.

In Colonial times the "poor debtors" in the Gaol were largely dependent for food upon the kindness of friends; for after the first twenty days of their imprisonment their creditors had to pay for their support. As the barred and inadequate window was unglazed and the sanitary arrangements primitive, the prison could hardly have been even a bearable place.

The Laws of Virginia demanded violent punishments and profitable fines; and to avoid the high cost of supporting criminals, the General Court usually fined, lashed, branded, mutilated, or hanged persons convicted. Half-savage Negroes, hardly civilized Indians, as well as unruly indentured servants, some of whom were transported felons, presented certain punitive problems to the judiciary.

Henry Maynard returned with the head of Black Beard dangling from the bowsprit of his victorious sloop and with fifteen of the piratical crew as prisoners. They were all thrown into the Williamsburg Gaol to await trial and afterwards hanged on the Capitol Landing Road.

Peter Pelham, the last Colonial keeper of the Gaol, was unanimously chosen organist of the Church. He also taught the young ladies of the Capital to play the harpsichord and spinet. Perhaps he had a tender heart as well, for he came up for investigation before the Assembly on the charge of allowing prisoners to escape. However, he was vindicated of the charge of taking money for his carelessness.

With the coming of the Revolution, the already crowded court calendars were swamped with new prisoners; for the turbulent public affairs added traitors, Tories, deserters, and spies to those awaiting trial. This condition, of course, soon resulted in a disastrous outbreak of pestilence, which resulted in many deaths before it was brought under control.

The restorers unearthed the major part of the foundations. Working with voluminous records and the standing building, which was an altered portion of the original Gaol, they were enabled to make a restoration of unusual authenticity.

54

THE PUBLIC GAOL

Reclaimed from some of its grimness, this cheery little building is now the "strong sweet Prison for Criminals" of Hugh Jones's time.

DEANE FORGE AND SHOP

Few horses now come to this watering trough, but the forge has a smith to work the bellows and send the sparks flying once again.

JACK MANLEY ROSÉ

BEHIND THE DEANE HOUSE at the junction of the Palace Green and Prince George Street is the forge and shop rebuilt by the Restoration as one of their buildings open to the public. Doubtless Elkanah Deane, who bought this fine property with its severely lovely house, conducted his coach and riding-chair business here. A great pity it is that no chairs or chaises of his making are known to exist to tell us of his skill. As he was patronized by the Governor, he must have turned out some worthy work in his time.

56

The house itself is foursquare and dignified, with white clapboarding and black-green shutters, and great symmetrical clumps of quick-growing box on each side of the doorway. Delicate wrought-iron railings suggest a charming bit of advertising for the forge in the rear, where iron work is still hammered out today for all to see, in accordance with the official craft program of the Restoration. In the years of its great activity turning out nails, relining sedan chairs, rimming wagon wheels, or making stirrups for gentlemen's saddles, Mr. Deane's forge must have been the busy and attractive place that loungers, small boys, and timid visitors have always found the old village smithy to be.

THIS INFORMALLY charming little cottage shop has been reconstructed on its original site over near the Capitol. At Governor Fauquier's death, Ann Ayscough, who had been the valued cook at the Palace in his time, was left a legacy which she and her husband Christopher, formerly a gardener at the Palace, probably used in opening a tavern and a shop. George Washington mentions the Tavern in his diary as being at Capitol Square and Francis Street.

Excellent cabinet work is being done today under the auspices of the Restoration in this shop and dwelling. The Sign of the Golden Ball on Duke of Gloucester Street and the Craft House adjacent to the Williamsburg Inn are open to the public also as part of a program to encourage participation in the fine arts and crafts of earlier days and to induce visitors to observe and purchase the really authentic furnishings that are designed and made in the old painstaking manner of the true craftsman.

THE WYTHE HOUSE was given by the builder and owner, Richard Taliaferro, along with a Negro wench, Peg; a boy, Joe; and £25 annually, to his daughter and her husband, George Wythe, and has since been known by the name of this eminent "Man of law." Richard Taliaferro, however, was himself a distinguished architect and builder, as is attested by the surviving examples of his work.

Chancellor Wythe, or Signer Wythe, as he has been called, was highly regarded as a lawyer, scientist, and designer of the Seal of the Colony of Virginia. He attended the College of William and Mary and after a youth supposedly spent in dissipation at the age of thirty he settled into a life of integrity and purpose. In later years he freed all his slaves and provided for their subsistence.

Prior to the Siege of Yorktown, General Washington made this residence on the Palace Green his headquarters. The house is as fine an example of Tidewater Domestic Colonial architecture, applied to a private dwelling inside and out, as exists today in Williamsburg. Its wide hospitable hall and broad sweeping staircase, its fine paneling and woodwork all give evidence of the grace and beauty of good living.

This house, for some reason as yet unrevealed, also has a monopoly on spectral visitors in the little city. George Wythe, who died by poison thought to have been administered by his nephew, returns in spirit from Richmond, where he spent his later years, to haunt the house he lived in so long. It is said on the anniversary of his death he lays a chill touch upon the face of whoever is sleeping in his bedroom. Some say George Washington appears on moonlit nights, his noble profile in strong silhouette against a window as he paces back and forth. Others claim that this ghost is Governor Page, who once owned the house, a gentle unobtrusive soul, wandering about harmlessly and quietly when the moon is full.

THE EASTERN STATE HOSPITAL presented the Travis House to the Restoration, which moved it across the intervening hollow to its present location on Duke of Gloucester Street. It was set on the foundations of a Colonial house once owned by John Greenhow, onto which it fitted surprisingly well. This journey across country took no less than two weeks.

Architecturally the Travis House is a typical dwelling of the vicinity, and antedates 1765. It is notable because of its bricked gable ends and gambrel roof. The sheathed wooden "ears" above the cornice are met by a slight tapering of the brickwork, and the dormer windows in the steep slope of the roof are exceedingly shallow. This type of roof was used in Williamsburg, it is said, to avoid the higher tax placed upon full two-storied dwellings. The window trim and sashes are largely original, and the shutters are partly new and partly old.

Utilized by the Restoration as an eating place where superlative Southern food may be obtained, it is by far the most atmospheric and satisfying of all the "Ordinaries" of Williamsburg. Dinner, tea, and supper are beautifully served either indoors or out-of-doors, on the porch or in the garden, according to the season and the weather.

The interior with much of the original woodwork has been faithfully decorated and is, in the manner of most of the Exhibition Buildings, regularly adorned with flower arrangements that have all the quality of old still-life paintings by Flemish masters. Appropriate, mixed bouquets of locally grown and cultivated flowers, fruits, and shrubs are used, as well as wild growth from the roadsides, the pastures, and the near-by woods.

The hostesses and servitors, unself-consciously attired in the dress of the 1750 period, are no less hospitable or efficient for that pleasant touch of by-gone color.

There is a green garden marked off by luxuriant holly hedges and containing secluded and shaded niches, as well as two white cupolaed and screened summerhouses where luncheon, tea, or dinner may be enjoyed. Old records show that at the hostelry which stood on this spot prior to the beginning of the nineteenth century long boards on trestles were sometimes set out under the trees in the garden for the pleasure of the guests.

WHERE THE ROAD up the Peninsula enters Williamsburg, Francis Street begins; and it is just about here, a little east of the Capitol, that the true quality of the old town is first evident. A number of delightful private homes are tucked away under the tree shadows; and as unspoiled and as old as any is the Benjamin Waller House. It became successively the property of Benjamin Waller's son and then of his grandson William, who married Elizabeth Tyler, daughter of President John Tyler. In later years it was owned by William E. Morecock, clerk of the James City County Court. His daughters continue to uphold its reputation for warm hospitality.

The grounds of the house extend far back and are adjacent to the property of Bassett Hall, occupied by the Rockefeller family when in residence in Williamsburg. At the rear of the Waller garden is a small private cemetery, walled about with the characteristic brick and molded coping of the locality. Some great trees, ivy-grown and all but choked, have thrust their roots under the wall to its detriment; and shafts of sunlight strike down through the leafy seclusion, dramatically to rest upon the mossy marble slabs over the graves of those who are reposing there.

The ancient well on the place brings to mind a romantic story that may or may not have had its inception here. Some years ago students calling at a home where there were several daughters found it exceedingly difficult, under the eye of a fond but rather particular father, to manage to see any of the girls alone. So it was tacitly agreed among the young people that if any swain indicated that he was thirsty, one of the girls would show him the way to the well, the cool water of which was always excuse enough even to the strictest parent for a stroll down the garden. So it chanced that during the course of an evening to allay the amazingly persistent thirst of their guests, the girls in turn steered an almost steady procession of favored young men down the path to the well. They had a carefully worked-out system to insure that their absences did not overlap and that each received his fair share. Under the magnolias, one can almost fancy the pale glow of summer dimities against the shadows and hear the slurring cadence of young Virginia voices rise and fall, broken by those sudden silences so fraught with magic. It is to be hoped that the fond parent never quite awoke to the realization of the pretty game, or, if he did, steadfastly refused to see anything unusual in the constant thirst that so regularly assailed all the young men of an evening.

THE BENJAMIN WALLER HOUSE

This unrestored house has never lost its pleasant hospitable charm. With its wide, cool hall and fine furnishings, it is typical of the homes of Williamsburg.

SHOPS ALTERNATING with dwellings, and Public buildings with Inns and Ordinaries add to the variety and color of Duke of Gloucester Street now even as they did in the past.

Here is a captivating bit of a building called the Greenhow Shop. It suggests indubitably a tuck shop of another century, and further along the street next to the Ludwell-Paradise House is the restored apothecary shop of Dr. Archibald Blair, a really charming little place that detracts not at all from the elegance of its neighbor.

A little shop at The Sign Of the Golden Ball, where at present an artificer in metals is working, is also on this street, not far from the Raleigh Tavern. In the busy days of Williamsburg's golden age many interesting things, such as punch and toddy ladles, cream buckets, piggins, caudle-cups, and silver buckles for both linen stocks and knee breeches, were made in this sort of shop.

In fact all the street is interspersed with these small and fascinating shops, and yet with its public buildings, church, and fine dwellings it is dignified and impressive. Some of these stores give one a strong desire to set up shop instantly. A wide window of small panes such as the Greenhow Shop possesses suggests jars of sweetmeats ranged on narrow shelves behind the glass. A tinkling bell would announce a customer, and from the little room behind the shop, where one could live, it would be fun to emerge (in Colonial dress, of course) and wait upon a possible buyer of some of the weird condiments, sweets, and baked goods of the day.

On the shelves would be jars of pickled nasturtiums, tomato soy, vinegar of the four thieves, pickled limes, and stone crocks of jumbals, macaroons, tavern biscuit, and apoquiniminc cakes. Syllabubs, flummery, and trifles and orgeat could be made to order; and hartshorn and currant jellies and choice Barbadoes sweetmeats in small pots would undoubtedly adorn the counter.

It is hard to realize as one strolls along these shady brick walks that at one time not so very long ago the sidewalks on this fine street were made of concrete and lined with telegraph poles, and that "here and there a leaning dormer or a handsome chimney cap offered the only visible identifying features which marked instances in which Colonial buildings had been swallowed up in Renovations and Repairs." Future generations will come to enjoy Williamsburg but they may never know the new from the old, the reconstructed from the dilapidated, the restored from the original.

JACK MANLEY ROSÉ

STREET SCENE: GREENHOW SHOP AND OTHERS

It is the homely little glimpses of architectural and gardening irregularities along these shaded sidewalks that endear restored Williamsburg to the visitor.

ST. GEORGE TUCKER, after whom the house is named, came to Williamsburg from Bermuda for schooling in 1772 and lodged with Mrs. Eustace, mother-in-law of James Blair, then Bursar of the College of William and Mary. Along with the other gay sparks of the College, he apparently joined the F. H. C., known to the uninitiated students as the Flat Hat Club. It is thought to have been a forerunner of Phi Beta Kappa and in fact of all college fraternities which have followed.

Young Tucker studied under George Wythe, as a sort of secretary-clerk, reading law with him, having the use of his library, and dining at his table. He seems to have been an impetuous, lavish, and popular young man throughout his college course. After graduation he was admitted to the bar but, thinking his chances for success better in Bermuda, he returned there. Eventually he found his way back to Williamsburg, this time to settle. After a considerable courtship, he married Frances Randolph, the widowed sister of his friend Theodorick Bland, the younger. Although she was only twenty-five, she was already the mother of three sons and the mistress of a large plantation.

Evidently Tucker engaged in trade with England for a while. There is a record of a certain order for finery given him by Mrs. Randolph before she consented to become Mrs. Tucker. He procured for her "a pair of stays agreeable to enclosed measure . . . of white sattin, tabby or ticken," and five pairs of shoes, two of "white sattin, 1 of blue, 1 of black, & 1 of pink."

The law finally won him back, and in time he became the successor of George Wythe in the professorship of law at the College of William and Mary. He was a great letter writer, a poet as well as a jurist, and the author of several dramas, both tragic and comic. John Adams had occasion to praise very highly one of his poems entitled *Days of My Youth*. He also won some fame as a political satirist and was a member of the Annapolis Convention in 1786.

A long line of prominent men and women have lived in this fine old house of massive chimneys, hospitable wings, and white gables set in a sea of great clumps of dark boxwood. The adjoining property, on which stood the first theater in The American Colonies, opened in 1716, and the "good Bowling Green," have been given by the former owners of the house to the Restoration.

The tradition of achievement which the first St. George Tucker in America established and which has been handed down through generations of St. George Tuckers to the present day gives an added interest to this house.

THE ST. GEORGE TUCKER HOUSE

"Bermuda me genuit,—Virginia fovit," *is the motto of the house of the earliest*
St. George Tucker in Virginia.

THE GARDEN of small boxwood lying between the John Custis Tenement and the James Galt House immediately attracts the passer-by. A huge tree with dappled bark dominates the garden area; and the silvery-gray branches of a great crape myrtle shrub twist into a lovely pattern of rhythmic growth, casting fantastic shadows over the crisscrossing paths. The small triangular plots edged with box are gay with iris, sweet William, and clove pinks in season; and ivy is trailed along the edges of the box so that when the blossoms are gone the garden is still verdantly green.

A letter from a John Custis, of Williamsburg, tells of the difficulties of the early gardening:

. . . Yᵉ box for my garden was all rotten as dirt did not save one sprig; yᵉ gardener was either a fool or a knave and by his management never packᵈ anything before to go beyond sea. . . . They should have had all the air imaginable, and bee set in yᵉ Chest as they should grow, instead of that they were laid atop of one another and nailᵈ close; I had rather bee disappointed in any one thing else . . .

But enough boxwood was successfully imported from England to Virginia during the Colonial period to enable the Restoration to rescue from impoverished river gardens and from about the deserted foundations of once stately homes of the Tidewater, at least a mile and a half of old hedges to adorn Williamsburg. Back of the Brush House on the Palace Green are most remarkable old bushes, carefully tended, sprayed, and braced by the Restoration's fine landscape gardeners. So fine are they that they are exceeded perhaps only by Gunston Hall's famous box walk.

The Custis House once had good lodgings for gentlemen on reasonable terms. It is now occupied by descendants of the Huguenot family of Gabriel Maupin. The original house burned accidentally in 1776 while Continental soldiers were quartered there.

The James Galt House, small, oak-framed, and irregular, originally stood on the grounds of The Eastern State Hospital, but was moved to its present location and set up in the place of a missing eighteenth-century dwelling.

THE JOHN CUSTIS TENEMENT

This is a reconstructed frame house put up on the site of the tenement (so-called because it was built for renting) owned by John Custis III.

THIS DWELLING with double front steps stands near the College and was probably built sometime between 1745 and 1747. The westerly end is of later construction.

The Blair family, always active in the life of Williamsburg and prominent in the history of the Virginia Colony, seem to have been of an exceptionally vigorous and lively temperament. The Reverend James Blair, the "Governor Breaker," who in his lifetime was responsible for having three Royal Governors recalled, and who acted as Governor himself in 1740-41, was one of them. John Blair, President of the Council, who lived in this house, was another. His daughter Anne, or Agan, as she is sometimes called, wrote in August 1769 the following delightful letter which is quoted from Mr. Rutherfoord Goodwin's *A Brief and True Report for the Traveller Concerning Williamsburg in Virginia:*

. . . Mrs. Dawson's Family stay'd ye Evening with us, and ye Coach was at ye Door to carry them Home, by ten o'clock; but everyone appearing in great Spirits it was proposed to set at ye Steps and Sing a few Songs, wch was no sooner said than done; while thus we were employ'd, a Candle or Lanthorn was observed to be coming up Street; (except Polly Clayton censuring their ill Taste, for having a Candle on such a fine Night) no one took any Notice of it —till we saw, who ever it was, stop to listen to our enchanting Notes—each Warbler was immediately silenced; whereupon the Invader to our Melody, call'd out in a most rapturous Voice, Charming! Charming! proceed for God Sake, or I go Home directly—no sooner were those Words uttered, than all as with one Consent sprung from their Seats, and ye air echo'd with "pray, Walk in my Lord"; No,—indeed he would not, he would set on the Step's too; so after a few ha, ha's, and being told what all knew—that it was a delightful Evening, at his desire we strewed the way over with Flowers &c &c. till a full half Hour was elaps'd when all retir'd to their respective Homes . . .

This so definitely expresses the spirit of the times during Lord Botetourt's regime and the tolerant, easy, half-affectionate regard in which he was held. One of the large stones incorporated in the steps of this house came from the site of the first theater in Williamsburg, according to local lore.

Also it is said that Chief Justice Marshall lived here for a short period, and from this door went forth—a kindly and lovable man but noticeably slovenly in his dress.

72

THE BLAIR HOUSE

It may have been on one of these stone steps that Anne Blair, Polly Clayton, and the Dawsons sang on a certain fine night in August, 1769, with Governor Botetourt as their audience.

HUGH ORR, for whom the house was named, was a prosperous blacksmith; and at his death the inventory shows that he left it handsomely furnished and with an excellent library for the times. The Restoration has taken it in hand and planted on the premises a delightful garden—one of the few open to visitors. One reaches it through a low white gate between this house and the Lightfoot residence next door. The garden itself is very unpretentious but has charming vistas. With its wide white garden benches, it is a friendly spot to sit in and rest a while. Like many Williamsburg gardens it is a shady, or green garden, planted with cool evergreens, whose shade is very welcome when the Virginia summer brings its "violent hot weather," as Hugh Jones stated over two centuries ago. An outstandingly lovely native wistaria vine has been trained with careless artfulness across the gable end of one of the outhouses, possibly the milk house or what in a New England garden would be the woodshed. A delightful shrub of crooked growth leans over the picket fence, and ancient moss lies between the bricks of the newly laid walks.

Everywhere is evident the careful but seemingly casual directing of the garden growth—lavish and ebullient foliage trained carefully into lines of beauty that nature itself could never have achieved in the few years that have elapsed since the planting was first undertaken.

More shops are constantly springing up along Duke of Gloucester Street. Across the lane that leads past the Orr outhouses and their whitewashed fences, to the new and not-too-harmonious-looking Inn, a row of brick dwellings has just been completed. Numerous buildings have been torn down in the area that constituted old Williamsburg and are being replaced by well-built and interesting edifices that research has determined might well have stood in the same places during the Colonial period. The careful building operations that go on here are a lesson in good craftsmanship. One can linger and watch the skill, judgment, and authenticity which enter into the workmen's training and rejoice that at least a few artisans and mechanics in this country are being encouraged in the old traditions of worth-while and enduring construction. Instructed in the best practices of the building trades, absorbing unconsciously the flavor of the past, and sharing the excitement of raising an enduring monument, the craftsmen work constantly in an environment of beauty and participate in the actual creation of it.

CAPTAIN ORR'S GARDEN

This sturdy dwelling in which Hugh Orr, blacksmith, lived in 1739, may have been before that the house of Edward Barradall, the Attorney General of the Colony.

JUST OPPOSITE the Capitol, at the very head of Duke of Gloucester Street, stands the fine old mansion known as the Kerr House. It burned in 1734 and the rebuilt house is probably somewhat larger than the original one. Vine-mantled as few of the Williamsburg buildings are, and shaded by tall trees, it has a shadowy grace, a height and dignity that set it apart from many of the other residences of more intimate charm.

The interior of the house has the usual wide and welcoming hall opening through to the sunny garden. The ceilings are lofty and the rooms spacious and well-proportioned. It is fortunate in much of its furniture which preserves the quality of other days and is exceedingly livable at the same time. It is a surprising but certainly comforting thought to realize that the furnishings and accouterments of those long past days still suit our ways of living so admirably.

The gardens of this house, on the corner of Blair Street and Duke of Gloucester Street are pleasantly varied and bright with sunlight, and the kitchen, restored, has a great deal of interest for the passer-by. Abutting as the gardens do on Capitol Square and shaded by a row of very old and twisted paper mulberry trees along the street line, it seems as if they had actually been there ever since the days when Alexander Kerr, goldsmith and jeweler, sold and raffled on these premises mother-of-pearl snuff boxes and gold toothpick cases.

Here on these grounds not far from the kitchen, a kiln was built; and brick was molded but not fired because the House of Burgesses meeting in the Capitol, across the Square, complained of the kiln before it had even been lighted.

Another kitchen of greater historical interest but less picturesque quality today, is the Martha Custis Kitchen, still standing on the property that was once the Custis Plantation but is now incorporated into the grounds of the Eastern State Hospital. It and one old yew tree are all that mark the ancestral home of Daniel Parke Custis, the first husband of that capable and bustling widow who later became Mrs. George Washington.

Tradition has it that in this very kitchen, the practical Martha Dandridge Custis, as she was then, measured out the provisions for the meals served in the great house to which she came as a bride, as was the custom of the day.

Another less likely legend in connection with this little building maintains that it was here that the bashful George Washington courted the sympathetic widow while he attended the Assembly Sessions in Williamsburg.

THE KERR KITCHEN

Two kitchens, one restored and one not restored, but both inseparably identified with the eighteenth century, are the Kerr Kitchen and the Martha Custis Kitchen.

THE MARTHA CUSTIS
KITCHEN